Dear readers, thank you for choosing this small book of some scribbled words over those warm chats in your inbox. Even for this short period of time you spent reading my words, I am thankful to you. As a fresher in the field of literature, my work may contain errors which I consider as my beauty spots. Hope you would also do the same.

ANTE MORTEM TALES

"SOME THOUGHTS NEED TO BE CLARIFIED, SOME ARE BARE"

SHAFEEQ SHAJAHAN

Contents

Foreword

I would like neither to defame nor hurt anyone's sentiments, whether it's religious or personal. If you found any of my words in this book as offensive / provocative, it is purely co incidental. The words in this work are purely fictional, it doesn't represent or claim to represent any events or personal history of any individual. Poetic liberty has been taken with facts or details in this book, it should not be interpreted as completely literal or historically accurate.

Preface

I would like to offer this page to my dearest friend and classmate, who passed away on the last December . I regret for not answering your call. It is the only time I curse for being asleep. You were there for me when I struggled, but I was never there for you. I hope you are enjoying a good time with new friends in heaven. Waiting to see you there.

Acknowledgements

Thanks for all those who stood with me through every part of my life. My family, friends, those strangers who gave me a helping hand in need, I sincerely thank all of you from the bottom of my heart. Thanks to the divine nature for giving me a wonderful childhood. I would cherish on every memory that made it happier. Thank you my loving mother, father, my dearest sister and my beautiful nephews and nieces. Thank you Sarath, Chandana, Sajid, Sumithra, Arjun, Ashiq and all those friends who shared a laugh with me. I would like to thank my teachers for letting me explore the unknown, without you this would be never possible.

Prologue

"The only time men is not selfish is in his grave. No one can weep on his own"

1. Butchers' shop

Being a butcher is not easy.
I've to wake up my roosters,
eat the same meat from last night.
May the leftovers nourish my skinny pigs.
A butchers' shop does never close.
So, I've to clean it up every dawn.
Splashing drops of yesterday's craft
have changed to stable stains.
I've to slaughter my own sleep.
I don't want to, but I have to.
It's easier to butcher a man
than these crawling orphans.
I've lost my kindness, love and longing.
How can one care after slitting dozens to death?
But it's too good to be here.
I have the potions of forever tranquility.
Even the lowest of souls
curse me for the same sorcery.

2. Foeticide

He was the worst tumor
She ever had.
But she carried the pain
with that same sunken smile.
Eventhough she got another
budding lump inside, her
indifference got no fluctuations.
She tried some drugs and
poison pills,
gave her only stinging cramps.
She shattered on her own pool.
Craving for a gasp of breath.
All those men, the warmth
and care flashed like a
soaring shot.
She could no more
be merry with this lump.
She saw her bed like a
darkened sun,
Slowly fading off like a
corpse in sea.

3. The tryst

Let's feast together.
Feast on our flesh and bones,
Feast on our blood and brain,
Feast on our hearts and souls.
Let's burp with joy.
Joy of feasting on the past,
Never let the hiccups throw up
our rotten memories.
Let's keep peace with our tummies.
Let it burn down the tears and worries.
May the sourness of happy times
Never hault our hunger.

4. Hamartia

He roamed across the deserts,
Cruised unknown seas,
Navigating the vague star
beyond his reach.
He got scars, bruises
And lethal cuts, but he never
stood back.
He pierced the raging
Storm, cut apart the seas.
Even the mighty
Atlas trembled on this
stubborn flesh.
He gulped the molten rocks,
hardened with
the cry of clouds.
Frozen lands and lost
spirits did fear his approach.
He neither bled nor sweat.
He roamed across the land
of ghosts and manes.
No weapon did win over him,
All his strength, stealth and wealth
Startled on that ominous day.

He stumbled on a dwarf willow,
Mute and silent all its life.
He thumped down with
a swollen cry.
He got a cut, in his gut.
It soared through his
rock like flesh.
All his virile, might and stout
surfled out, unfurled bare.
He bled enough to make
mighty atlantic fear.
The wrath in his gut,
Loathe in his brain and
Rage in his heart
Fluttered out as winged
beauties without nectar to live.

5. Vagrants

Swam through the swarms,
sewage and seas
bearing the burden of wrath,
arrogance and loathe.
In the brewery of thirst,
charm of the night forces the
thrust of my lust.
Worn and torn,
struggled to be born,
And of course !
"we all are born to
Grieve on others' grave".

6. The ligature

It was a dark and

dreadful night.

I was on my way back to graveyard.

I saw someone with the satan.

"Is this déjà vu?"

I wondered.

Luckily, I found the corpse

Swinging in the woods.

Lost and blind, he was

bleeding from his wounds.

Pathetic me !

Fed him with my rotten blood.

red and soft, but

Darkened with my acts of life.

He felt that pozy

Drink kicking then.

It made him threw up on that open woods.

"why is he still rude and crude?"

I got no response , hot and sultry

Breeze did blow.

Neither did i save his soul

Nor did i release the knot.

Let him join the tribe of manes.

7. Knot

Tried multiple ropes,
In the window bars,
In the ceiling hooks,
Even in the fat old oak tree.
but my brand new hammock never
got the dream swing.
Tried different knots,
From munter hitch to carrickbend.
It was never worth the try.
At last I took the last straw.
Let's try the gordian knot.
That too with that glistening neckchain.
Of course, it went south.
Foolish me! Tied up myself
Along with the chain.
It was not a cakewalk,
I struggled for the same breeze.
It was then I realized the harsh reality.
It was neither the rope nor the knot.
It was my own ardour
Which craved for the swing.
Let it find solace in the same sadist soul.

8. Deserted

The soaring showers
stormed across the sands
In search of his barren beauty.
Stretched miles across the globe,
Beyond the reach of his roaring storms,
She secluded herself
from his dizzy hands.
Swoon, lost and scorn,
His loathe, rage and wrath
tossed many ships, rigs and rafts.
She secluded in the shade
Of the scorching sun.
Blistering stones and melting sands
Tried healing the torn heart.
No breeze did blow,
No deity did shower
She remained barren in the
Blazing sun's nub.

9. Possession

He got possessed,
Not from the mundane evil spirits,
Dark eyed angels gave him burns,
cuts and wounds.
He concealed the pain,
the voice and the vision.
He gruelled in the
Middle of darkest nights,
No moon did care to shower
Him some beam.
He slowly started losing the strength,
Got shivers and violent sessions of vomits.
He got no desires, passions or dreams.
Only sunken eyes and puffed up skin.
May the lord never sue
This pious soul in his own court.

10. The woods wagon

He lay on the wet gravel,
stretched his stress out.
Shivering breeze from the woods
tingled up the bushes.
(Lord Zeus was still under
the weather that day)
Lying on the ground,
He shut his eyes .
Moonlit sky showered him bone chilling drops.
Cloudy corners covered the moon,
Dripping drops of chills.
His eyes – devoid of life
got no thrill in those sights.
it has already seen
many swords and blades.
No scene of barren death
now make him tremble.
After the creepy groan of midnight wolves,
He saw the rays of approaching doom.
Its grumpy noise shook up the earth,
slowly roaring through the sleeping woods.
He stood up straight
On the disfigured track

" I will still crave for you my love,
Even in my next million lives"

11. Deceased

She was the best part
of my mundane life.
We spent quality times.
together in the graves,
dump yards even in the
frozen death warmers.
We found ourself in
ghosted crowds.
We sat in the middle
of those purest humans ever.
All sleeping in white threads,
But still they got that enlighted hunger.
Soothing sun put on the sunny saffron shade,
Maybe to make up the mood
a little more drowsy.
We sip the dead stories of past,
Some painful, some pathetic.
It gives her the essence of eerie silence.
None of the spirits dare to break the same.
Even the Satan used to care her.
The scintillating scent of the
broken graveyards never scared her.
The death, demons and even

The lord of life would never
Let her go.

12. Homicide

None of them will resist.
How can someone already dead
resist a serene pleasure?
My scalpels have seen
more cadavers than a
rusted surgeons' knife.
My pen has pierced
more eyeballs than
the rich man's silver fork.
Dear lord, let my hammer
crack open more and more arts.
It was already drowned with a days' work.
Friend, please never let me down.
Let me serve my duty.
May the suffering souls
be soothed by my service.

13. Betrayal

Finally, he lost his balance.
The same rope which fed him
for the past 30 years
eventually betrayed him.
He used to dance upon it,
balancing his rusted heart
and sunken brain.
This rope was his hell and heaven.
It fed its' filthy owners
Till they threw up.
This saint juggled his worries
upon the strip of death.
It never failed to make them giggle.
It was a bare drop.
Straight up from the 30 feet.
He bear up the
death's divine delight.
It was his greatest show ever.
None of them could forget that night.
He made their jaws drop
atleast for this farewell show.

14. The attraction

Gravity has never failed
to amaze me.
I've seen many miracles,
from cradle to graveyard.
But none could match the
scintillating wit of attraction.
It has crushed some of my lads,
to flourish their blooming dreams.
It has torn many of my brothers,
Who tempted to sprint miles away.
Some of them defied the force,
I think it is the greatest boon,
a perfect companion, a hidden blessing.
Gravity has never failed to amuze me.
She arbitrates the struggles.
Suffocates those in need.
Warmth of life sickens some souls.
Chills won't be the same anymore.
My own heat startles me.
Let it fall with the wet,
unladen cold of earth.

15. Concealment

I carry my own corpse,
a rugged sack of rotten dreams.
Only lads of mine were burnt alive.
Now no bullets could struggle me.
No grenades or dagger
Can shiver me .
Don't count my comrades
with those fat bastards
who torn my brothers apart,
pierced my children alive.
I am both the birth and death,
May my gods never forgive
my divine deeds.
I only crave for the hell
Where I could rest at ease.

16. The perfect getaway

I won't settle in motels any more.
Those white sheets, perfectly
woven from purest of cottons.
It would trouble my sleep.
But the last one was different.
Beautifully knit and properly woven.
The pantry rolled out the bed,
scented with arabian oudh.
The bed was perfect,
rough and solid.
It got the soothing cold
of shades.

17. Dearest love

After so many thoughts,
My mind wandered out of bounds.
I'd never let your nobility down.
In the leaves of a fallen olive,
I saw you lie, dead but
Still you kept that undead smile.
Now, I realize,
I was the raven among the wolves.
Lean, lifeless who never
Let her die.
No threads of death could
Make you better.
I stood there stranded,
watching the vultures
feast on her.
I too got a slice of her.
A leftover gift from those aborning brutes.